The Golden Happy Birthday Book

Compiled by Barbara Shook Hazen   Illustrated by Rosalyn Schanzer

 GOLDEN PRESS • NEW YORK
Western Publishing Company, Inc.
Racine, Wisconsin

Golden, A Golden Book® and Golden Press® are trademarks of Western Publishing Company, Inc.
Library of Congress Catalog Card Number: 75-4415

ACKNOWLEDGMENTS

The compiler and publishers have made every effort to trace the ownership of all copyrighted material included in this anthology, and to secure permission from the holders of the copyright. In the event of any question arising as to the use of any of the selections, the publisher and the compiler, while expressing regret for any inadvertent error, will be glad to make the necessary correction in future printings. Thanks are due to the following publishers, publications, agents, owners of copyright, and authors for permission to reprint the material listed below:

"The Birthday Child" reprinted from *Round the Mulberry Bush* by Rose Fyleman by permission of Dodd, Mead & Company, Inc. and The Society of Authors. Copyright 1928 by Dodd, Mead & Company, Inc. Copyright renewed 1955 by Rose Fyleman.

A Birthday for Bird (text only) written and illustrated by Diane Redfield Massie. Text copyright © 1966 by Diane Redfield Massie. By permission of Parents Magazine Press.

"Mail" by Patty Sue Lumsden from *Story Parade*. Copyright 1951 by Story Parade, Inc. Reprinted by permission.

Seven Little Postmen by Margaret Wise Brown and Edith Thacher Hurd. Copyright 1952 by Western Publishing Company, Inc. Reprinted by permission.

"The Twins" from *Under the Tree* by Elizabeth Madox Roberts. Copyright 1922 by B. W. Huebsch, Inc. Copyright renewed 1950 by Ivor S. Roberts. Reprinted by permission of The Viking Press.

"Things I Like" from *The Friendly Book* by Margaret Wise Brown, copyright 1954 by Western Publishing Company, Inc. Reprinted by permission.

"If Johnny Could Whistle" by Bonnie Highsmith. Copyright © 1971, Highlights for Children, Inc., Columbus, Ohio.

"Goody O'Grumpity's Birthday Cake" by Carol Ryrie Brink, copyright 1937, copyright renewed 1965 by Story Parade, Inc. Reprinted by permission of the author.

"Birthday Cake" by Aileen Fisher from *Runny Days, Sunny Days*, published by Abelard-Schuman Limited, New York. Copyright © 1958 by Aileen Fisher. Reprinted by permission of the author.

"Little Dragon's Birthday" by Ann Devendorf. Copyright © 1968, Highlights for Children Inc., Columbus, Ohio.

"Present" by Miriam Clark Potter from *Golden Book of Little Verses*. Copyright 1953, Western Publishing Company, Inc. Reprinted by permission of the heirs of Miriam Clark Potter.

"The Witches' Birthday Party" by Frances Veirs from *Story Parade*. Copyright 1952 by Story Parade, Inc. Reprinted by permission.

"The End" from *Now We Are Six* by A. A. Milne, illustrated by Ernest A. Shepard. Copyright 1927 by E. P. Dutton & Co., renewal © 1955 by A. A. Milne. Reprinted by permission of the publishers, E. P. Dutton & Co., Inc. and Curtis Brown Ltd.

CONTENTS

THE BIRTHDAY CHILD

By Rose Fyleman

Everything's been different
  All the day long,
Lovely things have happened,
  Nothing has gone wrong.

Nobody has scolded me,
  Everyone has smiled.
Isn't it delicious
  To be a birthday child?

Monday's child is fair of face.
Tuesday's child is full of grace.

Wednesday's child is full of woe.
Thursday's child has far to go.

Friday's child is loving and giving.
Saturday's child works hard for a living.

But the child born on the Sabbath day
Is sunny and happy and good and gay.
——Old Rhyme

A BIRTHDAY FOR BIRD

By *Diane Redfield Massie*

"My BIRTHDAY'S next week!" said a bird,
Hoping his friends had all heard.
He'd told them at least twenty times every day,
Mentioning things in a casual way,
Like presents a bird most preferred.

"What shall I give him?" said Quail.
"All that I have is this snail.
The inside is gone, since I ate it last week,
Perhaps he could use it for resting his beak,
Or a basket for keeping his mail."

11

"I have a feather," said Wren,
"Which I usually use for a pen,
But it seems a bit silly and rather absurd,
To give him a feather when he is a bird,
Like giving an egg to a hen."

"I have a present," said Grouse,
"It's a beautiful sunflower blouse!
I made it myself from a flower I had.
Its buttons fell off, but it wouldn't look bad
For an awning on top of his house!"

"I haven't much," said a mole,
Pulling chicory roots from his hole,
"But maybe he might like this shiny black stone.
Perhaps it would make a nice bird telephone,
If tied to a telephone pole."

12

"The only thing I have," said Duck,
"Is this nail which fell off of a truck,
I have it tied onto the end of a string.
I use it for wishing for any old thing,
Who knows, it might bring him some luck."

"My birthday is coming," said Bird,
"I do hope the others have heard."
He worried at night that his friends would forget.
His birthday was coming but wasn't here yet.
"Perhaps they've forgotten," said Bird.

"My birthday," said Bird, "is TODAY!
But I haven't heard anyone say,
'Happy Birthday, dear Bird, Happy Birthday to you!'
I thought they'd remember a present or two.
Perhaps they have all gone away!"

13

The grouse and the duck and the quail,
Guiding the mole by the tail,
Whispered to Wren, who was ready to sing,
To bring out the presents hid under his wing,
And together they sang rather well.

"HAPPY BIRTHDAY, DEAR BIRD, HAPPY YOU!"

The bird hardly knew what to do.
"There are presents for me?" said the bird with surprise,
And he wiped away tears from the sides of his eyes.
"It's hard to believe that it's true."

"How lovely," said Bird to the quail.
"A basket for keeping my mail!
And here is a feather for dusting my nest;
I have several others, but this is the best!
And an excellent awning and nail!"

14

"How nice!" said the bird through his phone.
"It's something I've wanted to own.
I'll call you each up, if you haven't called me,
And invite you to come for crackers and tea,
I've never liked eating alone."

"HAPPY BIRTHDAY!" sang Bird, "HAPPY ME!
I've presents and crackers and tea!"

Then he served them all tea with his cup and his spoon.
And they danced and they sang almost all afternoon,
With the happiest bird that could be.

MAIL

By Patty Sue Lumsden

When the mailman stops,
  I race to see
If a letter's come
  Addressed to me.

When a package comes
  "Oh! What's inside?"
I can hardly wait
  Till it's untied!

SEVEN LITTLE POSTMEN

By Margaret Wise Brown
and Edith Thacher Hurd

A boy had a secret. It was a surprise.
He wanted to tell his grandmother.
So he sent his secret through the mail.
The story of that letter
Is the reason for this tale
Of the seven little postmen who carried the mail.

Because there was a secret in the letter
The boy sealed it with red sealing wax.
If anyone broke the seal
The secret would be out.
He slipped the letter into the mailbox.

The first little postman
Took it from the box,
Put it in his bag,
And walked seventeen blocks
To a big Post Office
All built of rocks.

The letter with the secret
Was dumped on a table
With big and small letters
That all needed the label
Of the big Post Office.

Stamp stamp, clickety click,
The machinery ran with a quick sharp tick.
The letter with the secret is stamped at last
And the round black circle tells that it passed
Through the cancelling machine
    Whizz — whizz — fast!

17

Big letters
Small letters
Thin and tall—
The second little postman
Sorts them all.
The letters are sorted
From East to West
From North to South.

"And this letter
Had best go West,"
Said the second
Little postman,
Scratching his chest.
Into the pouch
Lock it tight
The secret letter
Must travel all night.

The third little postman in the big mail car
Comes to a crossroad where waiting are
A green, a yellow, and a purple car.
They all stop there. There is nothing to say.
The mail truck has the right of way!
"The mail must go through!"

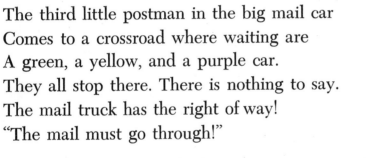

Up and away through sleet and hail
This airplane carries the fastest mail.
The pilot flies through whirling snow
As far and as fast as the plane can go.

And he drops the mail for the evening train.
Now hang the pouch on the big hook crane!
The engine speeds up the shining rails
And the fourth little postman
Grabs the mail with a giant hook.

The train roars on
With a puff and a snort
And the fourth little postman
Begins to sort.

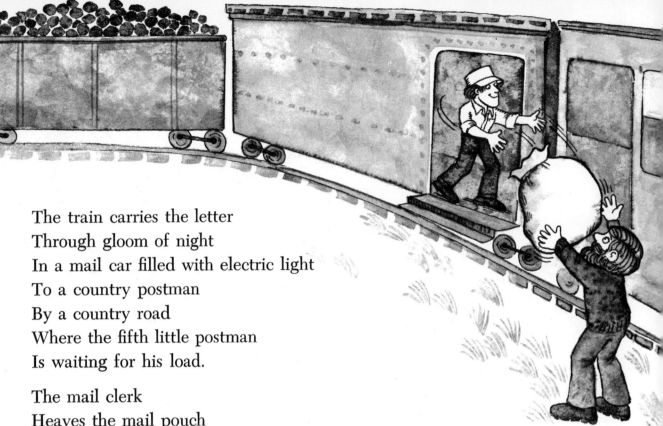

The train carries the letter
Through gloom of night
In a mail car filled with electric light
To a country postman
By a country road
Where the fifth little postman
Is waiting for his load.

The mail clerk
Heaves the mail pouch
With all his might
To the fifth little postman
Who grabs it tight.

Then off he goes
Along the lane
And over the hill
Until
He comes to a little town
That is very small —
So very small
The Post Office there
Is hardly one at all.

The sixth little postman
In great big boots
Sorts the letters
For their various routes —
Some down the river,
Some over the hill.

But the secret letter
Goes farther still.

The seventh little postman on R.F.D.
Carries letters and papers, chickens and fruit
To the people who live along his route.
He stops to deliver some sugar
To Mr. Jones who keeps a store
And always seems to need something more.

For Mrs. O'Finnigan with all her ills
He brings a bottle of bright pink pills.

An overweight letter that cost nineteen cents
He hands to a farmer over the fence.

There was a special delivery
Crisp orange and blue.
What was the hurry, nobody knew.

There were parts for a tractor
And a wig for an actor
And a funny post card
For a little boy
Playing in his own backyard.
There was something for Sally
And something for Sam
And something for Mrs. Potter
Who was busy making jam.

There were dozens of chickens
For Mrs. Pickens
And a dress for a party
For Mrs. McCarty.

At the last house along the way sat the grandmother of the boy who had sent the letter with
the secret in it. She had been wishing he
would come to visit. For she lived all alone in a
tiny house and sometimes felt quite lonely.

The Postman blew his whistle and gave her the
letter with the red sealing wax on it—the secret
letter!

"Sakes alive! What is it about?"
Sakes alive! The secret is out!
What does it say?

Dearest Granny:
I am writing to say
that I'm coming to
visit on your birthday.
My cat has seven kittens
and I am bringing one
to you for your very own
kitten.
The postman is my
friend.   Your grandson,
Thomas
xoxox

PARTY PIG

By Kathryn and Byron Jackson

One day it was Little Pig's birthday, and he was one year old.

He had new red overalls that fit just right, a new blue rocking chair that rocked high and low, and a new white handkerchief.

And that wasn't all.

The pantry in Little Pig's house was jammed and crammed with everything for a dandy birthday party — everything but a birthday cake.

But at that very moment Little Pig's mother was on her way to market to get some flour, so she could bake a cake for him.

And Little Pig was rocking away and thinking about that cake.

"It'll be big and high," he said dreamily. "With thick pink icing and thin pink candles and bright shiny lights on top of every single one!"

Just as Little Pig said that, he heard someone squeak, "I'm hungry!" in a sad way.

Down the path, leaning on a little red wheelbarrow, was a small, thin mouse. It was such a hungry-looking mouse that Little Pig ran into the pantry and brought out the whole party cheese and every bit of party candy.

"There, Mouse!" he said. "How's that?"

Then he called, "Come to my birthday party! Six sharp! Games and prizes!"

"I'll be there!" called the mouse.

23

No sooner had the gate closed than Little Pig heard a sad mewing sound from the bushes.

"I'm hungry, too," sobbed a small, striped kitten.

Little Pig ran into the pantry again.

This time he brought out all the tuna-fish salad, the whole big pitcher of milk, and all the cream.

The kitten gobbled up all that and thanked Little Pig.

"Come back for my birthday party," he called after her. "Six sharp, and there'll be games and prizes!"

Soon a whole parade of hungry people came into Little Pig's house.

A ragged puppy trotted up, crying for some meat.

A stickly porcupine bumbled up, moaning because he had no sugar for baking.

A skinny calf stumbled up, crying for some apples. And a sad, woolly lamb wandered up, bleating for some greens.

And then a shabby boy walked slowly up the path, wishing for some bread with butter and jelly.

Little Pig felt sorry for all those thin, hungry people!

He ran in and out of the pantry, giving them all of his birthday goodies. He asked every single one to come back for his birthday party, too.

They all went away, smiling and skipping

and hugging their packages. There was nothing left but twelve white eggs in a basket.

And those he gave to a sorry-looking hen who knocked at the door and said, "Deary, deary me! I'm going to be done away with because I can't lay eggs!"

Little Pig then hurried into the dining room to make some prizes. He made them out of paper and paste and crayons and pins.

He set the table, too, and hummed, "Happy Birthday to me, Happy Birthday to us, Happy Birthday to party — I love all this fuss!"

Little Pig was making his last prize when his mother came home.

When she saw the kitchen she cried, "Little Pig! Every last bit of your birthday dinner is gone!"

"Yes, Mother," said Little Pig. "I gave everything away — I guess."

"Oh, Little Pig!" his mother cried. "It's fine to be generous. But now we can't have a party."

"No party?" whispered Little Pig in a shaky voice. "Not even a cake?"

"Not even a cake," said Little Pig's Mother. "I can't make a cake with nothing but flour."

Poor Little Pig! He looked at his prizes. He looked at the table. He thought of all the people he had invited for six o'clock sharp. Then he sat down and cried.

Then, just as the clock struck six, voices

began to sing, "Happy Birthday, Little Pig!"

The door flew open. In came the mouse, his little wheelbarrow piled high with lollipops and peppermint sticks.

Next came the kitten with a fish, and the puppy with a whole roast turkey.

The porcupine had hot rolls, the calf carried a pitcher of milk, and the lamb brought cinnamon applesauce.

The hen carried a little pie she baked herself with "Little Pig" cut deep into the crispy crust.

Last of all came the boy. He had an enormous cake with thick pink icing and thin pink candles shining all over it.

Little Pig was so surprised and happy he couldn't say a word. He kissed his mother and hugged his friends. And then the party began.

Everyone ate, and joked, and laughed. It was a wonderful feast.

Afterwards, the games began. Then Little Pig gave out the prizes.

And it just turned out that, in one game or another, everyone who was at the party won a First Prize!

THE TWINS

By Elizabeth Madox Roberts

The two-ones is the name for it,
And that is what it ought to be,
But when you say it very fast
It makes your lips say *twins*, you see.

When I was just a little thing,
About the year before the last,
I called it two-ones all the time,
But now I always say it fast.

INDIAN INDIAN

By Charlotte Zolotow

This is a story about a whole family of Indians — a mother Indian, a father Indian, a brother Indian, a sister Indian, and a very little one named Indian Indian.

They all had horses but Indian Indian. And he wanted one more than anything in the world. He wanted one for his birthday.

One day, at breakfast time, Chief Rising Sun said, "As I came over the meadow this morning, just after dawn, the sun was so bright I almost believed I saw a horse lying in the grass.

"But no one would leave his horse in the meadow all night, so I realized it must be a trick of the eye, for the early morning sunlight will often trick the eye. Remember that, little one," he ended.

Little Indian Indian thought of what his father said. And after breakfast he set off to see if his eyes would trick him, too. He walked until he came to the meadow that sparkled with white daisies in the sun.

And there his eyes tricked him, too. Indian Indian walked closer and suddenly he saw that it was not a trick of his eyes at all. There was a great white horse lying in the daisies.

Very gently Indian Indian put out his hand and stroked the big horse. Then he put his arm around the horse's head and hugged the horse.

Perhaps this horse can't walk, thought Indian Indian. Then he would be thirsty.

29

So Indian Indian marched over to the brook. He found the bucket the Indians kept there. Indian Indian filled it with water and trudged back to the horse again.

The horse was thirsty. He drank as far down as he could reach.

Perhaps he is hungry, too, Indian Indian thought.

So he brought the horse some purple clover — as big an armful as his small arms could hold. The horse ate hungrily and looked at Indian Indian with grateful eyes.

Indian Indian then had to go home. "I'll be back," he said, stroking the horse's big head once again.

And off he went.

All day Indian Indian was busy with his work at home. But after dinner, when everyone had gone to sleep, little Indian Indian lay awake in the dark, thinking of his horse.

When the sun went down it would be cold. And Indian Indian shivered, thinking of how cold it must feel to lie there in the tall wet daisies with the darkness all around.

At last he got up. He took his warm woven blanket off the ground and tiptoed very quietly out of the hut.

The darkness around him seemed very big. The stars in the sky seemed cold and far away. There were strange noises across the meadows.

Indian Indian was frightened. But he thought of his horse, and went on through the whispering night.

He found the horse in the dark and stroked him. "I'm here," he said. "Don't be afraid."

He covered the shivering horse with his own wool blanket. Then he crept under it, too, and fell asleep.

In the morning, when everyone woke in the hut, there was no Indian Indian rolled up in his blanket on the floor. So they all set out to search.

And when they came to the meadow of white daisies, they saw — their eyes didn't trick them! — a big white horse sleeping under Indian Indian's wool blanket, with Indian Indian's own black head snuggled into the horse's fur.

They woke Indian Indian up.

"He is not a trick of the eye, Chief Rising Sun," said Indian Indian. "And I was afraid he was cold."

Chief Rising Sun smiled. He was happy to find his little Indian safe. He was pleased that Indian Indian had come through the darkness to his horse.

"You were wise, Indian Indian," his father said, "to test with your own senses what I had told you."

They examined the great white horse and found he had an injured leg. Chief Rising Sun put a bandage on it. Now the horse could hobble on his three legs until his fourth leg was better.

"Oh, please may I keep him?" said Indian Indian anxiously. "My birthday will be soon."

Chief Rising Sun looked down and smiled.

"Since you found him and fed him and brought him water to drink, and came in the night with a warm blanket, Indian Indian, the horse is rightfully yours," the father said.

The big horse nuzzled his wet nose gratefully into Indian Indian's hand.

They all started slowly across the fields toward home.

Indian Indian's heart was pounding with joy, and his eyes were shining like the sun.

Now everyone in the Indian family had a horse — Indian Indian, too. And that was what he wanted more than anything else in the world.

ANIMAL ORCHESTRAS

By Ilo Orleans

In Animal town
It was a special day.
The orchestra
Had gathered to play.
Everyone came
To hear and to see.
The big sign said,
ADMISSION FREE!
Up to the platform
Each animal went,
And proudly carried
His instrument.

They whistled! They fiddled!
They thumped! They blew.
What a roar! What a din!
What a great to-do!
The animal girls—
The animal boys—
The animal audience
Made a great noise.
They slapped their tails,
They clapped their paws,
And that is how
They made applause!

The conductor bowed,
And bowed and bowed.
All of the orchestra
Players were proud.
The Hippo was happy
On his special day,
For everyone shouted
"*Hip-HIPPO-ray!* and
HAPPY BIRTHDAY!"

THINGS I LIKE

By Margaret Wise Brown

I LIKE CARS.
Red cars, green cars,
Sport limousine cars,
I like cars.
A car in a garage,
A car with a load,
A car with a flat tire,
A car on the road.
I like cars.

I LIKE TRAINS.
Express trains,
Toy trains,
Streamline trains,
Freight trains,
Old trains,
Milk trains,
Any kind of train.
A train in the station,
Trains crossing the plains,
Trains in a snowstorm,
Trains in the rain,
I like trains.

I LIKE SEEDS.
Mustard seeds, radish seeds,
Corn seeds, flower seeds,
Any kind of seed.
Seeds that are sprouting green from the ground
And seeds of the milkweed flying around.
I like seeds.

I LIKE BUGS.
Black bugs, green bugs,
Bad bugs, mean bugs,
Any kind of bug.
A bug in a rug,
A bug in the grass,
A bug on the sidewalk,
A bug in a glass.
I like bugs.
Round bugs, shiny bugs,
Fat bugs, buggy bugs,
Big bugs, lady bugs.
I like bugs.

I LIKE FISH.
Silver fish, gold fish,
Black fish, old fish,
Young fish, fishy fish,
Any kind of fish.
A fish in a pond,
A fish in a stream,
A fish in an ocean,
A fish in a dream.
I like fish.

I LIKE DOGS.
Big dogs, little dogs,
Fat dogs, doggy dogs,
Old dogs, puppy dogs,
I like dogs.
A dog that is barking over the hill,
A dog that is dreaming very still,
A dog that is running wherever he will,
I like dogs.

I LIKE BOATS.
Any kind of boat.
Tug boats, tow boats,
Large boats, barge boats,
Sail boats, whale boats,
Thin boats, skin boats,
Rubber boats, river boats,
Flat boats, cat boats,
U-boats, new boats,
Tooting boats, hooting boats,
South American fruit boats,
Bum boats, gun boats,
Slow boats, row boats.
I like boats.

I LIKE WHISTLES.
Wild whistles, bird whistles,
Far-off heard whistles,
Boat whistles, train whistles,
I like whistles.
The postman's whistle,
The policeman's whistle,
The wind that blows away the thistle.
The little birds that whistle and sing,
And the little boy whistling in the spring.
The wind that whistles through the trees
And blows the boats across the seas.
I like whistles.

I LIKE PEOPLE.
Glad people,
Sad people,
Slow people,
Mad people,
Big people,
Little people.
I like people.

IF JOHNNY COULD WHISTLE

By Bonnie Highsmith

If Johnny could whistle, he could call his dog when it ran away. But he couldn't whistle, so his dog ran away every day.

Johnny would call, "Here, Topper. Here, Topper. Come, boy."

But Topper did not hear, so he didn't come back.

Johnny would make his lips into a little circle and blow. All that came out was a sputter.

If Johnny could whistle, he could teach his bird to sing. But he couldn't, so his bird just sat in his cage all day not making a sound.

Johnny would say, "Sing, Sunbeam. Sing. Tweet, tweet."

But Sunbeam did not understand, so he just sat on his perch and looked at Johnny.

Johnny would pucker up his lips and blow. All that came out was a puff of wind.

If Johnny could whistle, he could be the policeman when the boys and girls on the block played stop-and-go. But he couldn't, so someone else always got to be the policeman.

Johnny would shout, "Stop! Halt! Red light!"

But Bobby's wagon would keep on going. Freddy's trike would keep on going. Betty Lou's doll buggy would keep on going.

Johnny would puff up his cheeks and blow. All that came out was a funny squeak.

On his birthday, Johnny jumped out of bed all excited. "Today I'm six," he said. "Now maybe I can whistle."

Everyone he knew who was six could whistle. Bobby was six and he could whistle. Freddy was six and he could whistle. Betty Lou was only four and she could whistle.

All day he tried. All that came out was a sputter, a puff of wind, and a funny squeak.

Johnny's mother made a big, pink birthday cake. When it was time to blow out the candles, he took a *deep, deep, deep* breath and blew. Out went four candles, and — out came a loud, shrill whistle!

Johnny was so surprised that he forgot to blow out the rest of the candles.

He could whistle! Now he could call his dog when it ran away. He could teach his bird to sing. And he could be the policeman when the boys and girls played stop-and-go.

GOODY O'GRUMPITY'S BIRTHDAY CAKE

By Carol Ryrie Brink

When Goody O'Grumpity baked a cake,
The tall reeds danced by the mournful lake,
The pigs came nuzzling out of their pens,
The dogs ran sniffing and so did the hens,
And the children flocked by dozens
   and tens.

They came from the north, the east and the south
With wishful eyes and watering mouth,
And stood in a crowd about Goody's door,
Their muddy feet on her sanded floor.
And what do you s'pose they came to do!
Why, to lick the dish when Goody was through!

And throughout the land went such a smell
Of citron and spice — no words can tell
How cinnamon bark and lemon rind,
And round, brown nutmegs grated fine
A wonderful haunting perfume wove,
Together with allspice, ginger and clove,
When Goody but opened the door of her stove.
The children moved close in a narrowing ring,
They were hungry — as hungry as bears in the spring;
They said not a word, just breathed in the spice,
And at last when the cake was all golden and nice,
Goody took a great knife and cut each a slice.

46

BIRTHDAY CAKE

By Aileen Fisher

If little mice have birthdays
(and I suppose they do)

And have a family party
(and guests invited too)

And have a cake with candles
(it would be rather small)

I bet a birthday *cheese* cake
would please them most of all.

BIRTHDAY TWISTER

Birthday Betty bought some butter.
"Boy," said she, "this butter's bitter.
If I put it in my batter,
it will make my batter bitter.
But a bit of better butter
will but make my batter better."
So she bought a bit of butter
better than the bitter butter,
and made her bitter batter better.
So 'twas better Birthday Betty
bought that bit of better butter.

A BIRTHDAY CAKE FOR EVERY SEASON

Spring

Decorate your cake with tiny paper umbrellas. Or circles of candy-covered chocolates. Or with flowers, using pastel mints for flower centers and petals.

Summer

Circle your cake with festive flags. Or rolled kraft-paper firecrackers. Or daisies made from chocolate or butterscotch bits.

Fall

Add a black cat made from black gumdrops. Or write your name or age in candy corn or maraschino cherries. Or ring your cake with a hard-candy wreath.

Winter

Top your cake with a jolly fat marshmallow snowman. Or draw on a large red heart with candy redhots. Or make shamrock shapes with green gumdrops.

LITTLE DRAGON'S BIRTHDAY

By Ann Devendorf

Once upon a time there lived a dragon.
He was a very little dragon.
He lived with his mother and father.
They lived in the great woods.

Father Dragon puffed red fire.
Mother Dragon puffed blue fire.
Little Dragon puffed orange fire.

It was Little Dragon's birthday.
Mother Dragon said,
"I've made a birthday cake for you.
You may run and look for your friends.
Tell them to come and have
some birthday cake."

"Thank you!" said Little Dragon.
He ran into the woods.
He found Miss Mousie.
"It's my birthday," said Little Dragon.
"Come and have some birthday cake."

"Thank you," said Miss Mousie.
"I'd like to come.
But tell me something, please.
With your breath of fire,
how do you blow out your candles?"

"Wait and see," said Little Dragon.

Little Dragon found Lolly Lizard.
"It's my birthday," said Little Dragon.
"Come and have some birthday cake."

"Thank you," said Lolly Lizard.
"I'd like to come.
But tell me something, please.
With your breath of fire,
how do you blow out your candles?"

"Wait and see," said Little Dragon.

Little Dragon found Ole Turtle.
"It's my birthday," said Little Dragon.
"Come and have some birthday cake."

"Thank you," said Ole Turtle.
"I'd like to come.
But tell me something, please.
With your breath of fire,
how do you blow out your candles?"

"Wait and see," laughed Little Dragon.

He ran through the woods.
Miss Mousie, Lolly Lizard,
and Ole Turtle ran after him.

50

Mother Dragon put the cake on the table.
They all sat down.
"Make your wish, Little Dragon,"
said Mother Dragon.
Little Dragon made his wish.

He did not tell his wish.

Then he blew.
He blew a big breath of fire.
He lit every candle on the cake!

"Oh," laughed his friends.
"Now we know what dragons do.
They don't blow out candles
on birthday cakes.
They blow them on!"

"Yes," laughed Little Dragon.
"That's what we do.
And I got my wish, too."

MOLLY'S HAPPY BIRTHDAY

Adapted from a story by Elsa Ruth Nast

Molly's birthday is coming. She's going to have a party. Molly and her mother are making things for the party themselves.

"First, we must invite my friends," says Molly.

So Molly and her mother make invitations. Molly cuts out all the invitations. She cuts them out of light colored paper and draws designs on the front.

Here are several for you to copy.

Each invitation says inside:

Please come to my birthday party on (date) at (time) at (address). Please call (phone number) and let me know if you can come.

Mother writes most of the invitations. Molly signs her own name.

Molly folds the invitations neatly and puts them into envelopes. On each envelope Mother puts the name and address of one of Molly's friends. She puts her own address in the upper left corner.

Molly puts on the stamps in the upper right corner.

Then Molly drops the invitations into the mailbox.

52

"We'll need place cards, too," says Mother. So Molly and Mother make those.

Each place card is an animal shape. Each has ends to fold back and a blank place for the name.

Molly copies the designs or makes up some of her own. Then she colors them herself. And writes the name of each friend in the white space.

Here are some for you to copy.

FOLD ON DOTTED LINE

WRITE NAME HERE

FOLD ON DOTTED LINE

ELLEN

SAMMY

ADAM

BECKY

"What else do we need?" asks Mother.

"Cups for candy," says Molly. Mother helps Molly cut down and decorate paper drinking cups. They paste a colored paper handle on each cup. Then they fill them with gumdrops and jelly beans.

"Planning a party is fun," says Molly. "What shall we do now?"

"Let's make some colored paper chains to decorate the table," says Mother.

Mother shows Molly how to make the chains. Molly carefully cuts the colored paper into equal size strips, about 4 inches long.

She makes a ring out of each strip and fastens it with sticky tape. She takes a second strip, links it into the first, and fastens the ends. Soon she has made a long colorful chain that winds around the table.

Mother shows Molly how to make glitter balls too. "It's easy," says Mother. 1.) "Just cut six cellophane straws in half. 2.) Tie a string around the twelve pieces in the middle. 3.) Then pull the string tight."

"Easy and pretty," says Molly. "The straws spread out in all directions. She hangs the glitter ball by the leftover string.

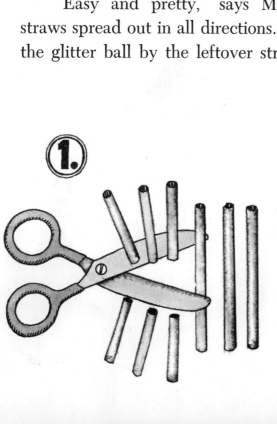

Now it is party time. All Molly's friends arrive. They bring presents for Molly. Molly opens them. Then they play games.

First they play *Pin - the - Tail - on - the - Donkey*.

Then they have a *Pirate Treasure Hunt*. Molly has hidden pennies under cushions and behind chairs. Everyone hunts. The one who finds the most "Pirate Gold" gets a prize. Everyone is allowed to keep his pennies.

They play *Poor Kitty* too. The person who's "it" goes to each guest and meows three times. The guest must pat Poor Kitty's head three times. Poor Kitty makes faces and does silly things and tries to make the other person giggle. The first person who does, is the next Poor Kitty.

The last game is *Birds Fly, Dogs Bark*. Molly is the first leader. She flaps her arms and says "Birds fly." Her friends must follow her commands, *unless* she calls out something that isn't so, such as, "Rabbits fly," or "Birds swim." Anyone who follows a false command has to drop out. The last person left becomes the next leader.

Now it is time to eat. This is the best time of all.

Molly has made up a game for marching to the table. Her friends line up. She gives each a cut-out marker with the same animal shape that is on that friend's place card.

All the guests march around the table till they find their places. The girl with the puppy marker sits where the puppy place card is. And so on.

When all Molly's friends see the pretty things to look at and the good things to eat on the table, they say, "Happy birthday, Molly! This is the best party ever!"

After the party, Molly helps Mother clean up. Then she writes down the names of her guests and what each brought. Right here.

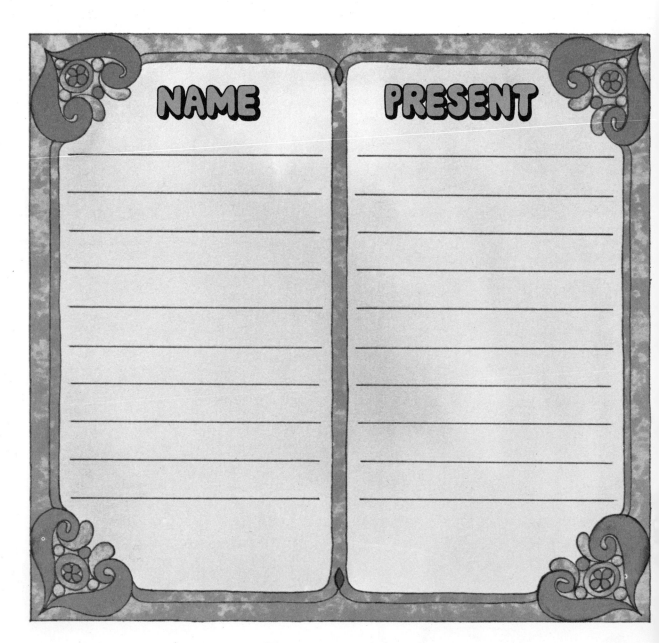

NAME PRESENT

PARTY FAVORS YOU CAN MAKE

By Florence Temko

CANDY BASKET

What you need:

A piece of gift-wrap paper, 5 inches square
A strip of gift-wrap paper, 1½ inches x 9 inches
(Use the paper double, if it is thin)

What you do:

1. Fold one bottom corner of the square to the opposite top corner. Unfold.

2. Fold the other bottom corner to the opposite top corner. Unfold.

3. Fold the side edges of the square to the center and unfold.

4. Fold the top and bottom edges to the center and unfold.

5. Pinch the four corners and staple or glue each one. Crease the corners sharply.

6. Fold the 9-inch strip of paper in half lengthwise and staple or glue it to the basket to make a handle.

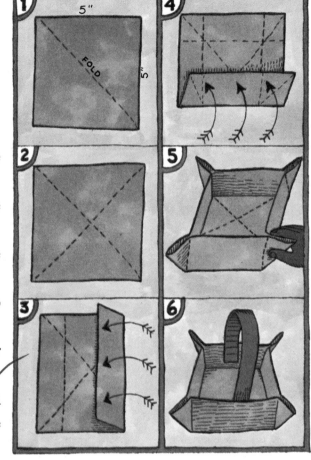

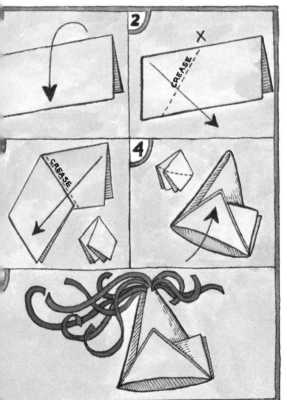

A BIRTHDAY HAT

What you need:

A piece of tissue paper, 30 inches x 20 inches
Another piece of tissue paper *(same size)*
in a different color.

What you do:

1. Fold one piece of tissue paper in half lengthwise.

2. Fold the left corner down as shown. Crease starts at X, which is the middle of the folded edge of the paper.

3. Then fold the right corner over.

4. Fold all layers of the bottom corner as far as they will go.

5. Cut strips of paper in different color tissue paper and staple them on the hat.

PRESENT

By Miriam Clark Potter

Mary Ann
Bought a box
At the shop;
And she went home;
She did not stop.

She went past the gate,
She went past the tree,
Three pink pigs,
And the grocery;

When she got home,
She gave the box
To Brother. He was
Playing with blocks.

It was a birthday
Present, you see.
He opened it
    AND
       OUT
          FELL
            ME!

PARTY PRIZES YOU CAN MAKE

A YARN DOLL

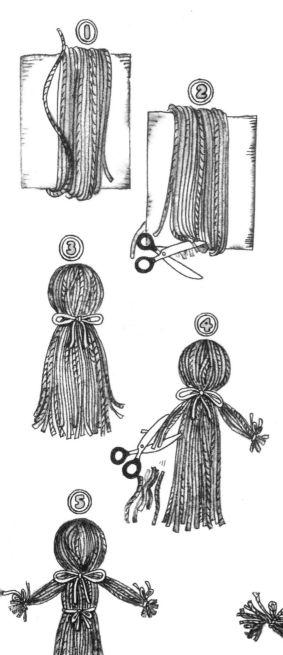

What you need:

Yarn *(any color)*
Cardboard *(Shirt cardboard works perfectly)*

What you do:

1. Wrap the yarn around and around the cardboard. The length of the cardboard will be the length of the doll.

2. Cut all the strands at the bottom end of cardboard. Remove from cardboard.

3. Plump the top strands into a ball. That's the head. Tie a separate piece of yarn where the neck should be.

4. Separate a few strands of wool on each side and cut them to make them the right length for arms. Tie yarn pieces where the wrists should be.

5. To make the body, bulge out the rest of the strands. Tie a yarn piece at the bottom of the body.

6. Divide the rest of the yarn in two to make the legs. To make the feet, tie two more yarn pieces around the "ankles" and two more near the ends.

A SQUIRMY SNAKE

What you need:

6 empty spools
About 2 yards of thick yarn or heavy cord
Beads
Optional: **paint or crayons or colored pens to decorate the spools**

What you do:

1. Tie a big strong knot at one end of the yarn or cord.

2. String the spools and beads in any pattern that pleases you. Add buttons between the beads if you wish.

3. Decorate the spools — draw or paint on them.

4. Tie another knot 2 inches after the last spool or bead.

Leave several feet of extra string for pulling. Make a finger loop at the end.

60

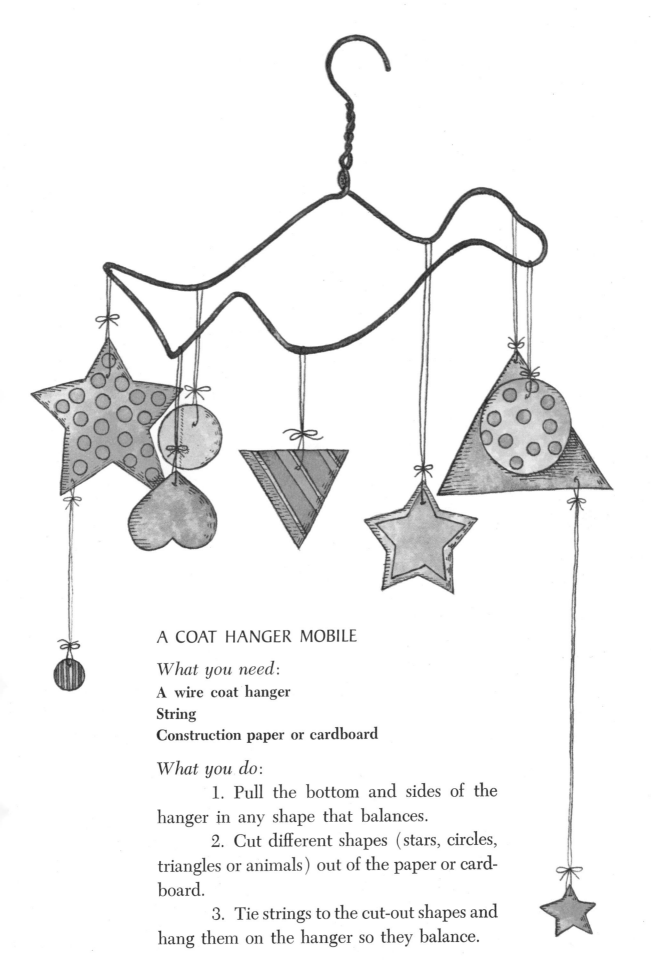

A COAT HANGER MOBILE

What you need:
A wire coat hanger
String
Construction paper or cardboard

What you do:

    1. Pull the bottom and sides of the hanger in any shape that balances.

    2. Cut different shapes (stars, circles, triangles or animals) out of the paper or cardboard.

    3. Tie strings to the cut-out shapes and hang them on the hanger so they balance.

GAMES TO PLAY
AT YOUR BIRTHDAY PARTY

Have a different colored string or yarn strand for each guest. Ask each guest to follow the string path to a surprise package. The more the string winds around, the more fun everybody has.

Have a nutty race. Everybody tries to roll a peanut across the floor with his nose. The winner gets a whole bagful.

Play the gossip game. One person passes a saying or piece of news on to his neighbor. The neighbor whispers it to the next person. When the "news" gets back to the first person, he tells what his neighbor told him and then what he really said at the beginning of the game. The longer the sentence, the funnier the changes will be. For instance, "Did you hear that Peter invited three spiny porcupines and an anteater to his birthday party?"

THREE WAYS TO TELL FORTUNES

FISH FOR IT

Write "fortunes" on pieces of paper. "You'll meet a frog who's really a prince," or "Look for lost pennies," or "A friend will say something nice about you," or whatever.

Fold the pieces of paper and put them into a bowl. Let every birthday guest pick out his or her fortune and read it aloud.

FIND IT IN THE CARDS

Lay out five cards in a row. Tell your friends' fortunes. Spades mean disappointment, hearts mean love, diamonds mean riches, clubs mean hard work. Kings are handsome men, queens are beautiful women, and jacks are children.

PULL IT OUT OF A GRAB BAG

Put an assortment of fortune-telling keepsakes into a bowl. Each friend closes his eyes and dips into the bowl. He can tell his fortune by the piece he touches first.

For instance, a penny means wealth; a ring, romance; a nail, hard work; a toy car, travel; an envelope, a letter coming soon in the mail.

What is the birthday boy after he is five years old?

Six years old.

What kind of birthday bow is it impossible to tie?

A rainbow.

What looks like half a birthday cake?

The other half.

What kind of dog has no tail and goes to birthday parties?

A hot dog.

How did George Washington celebrate his birthday?

How would I know. I wasn't invited.

Why did the birthday girl toss the clock out the window?

To see time fly.

How would you light birthday candles with two sticks?

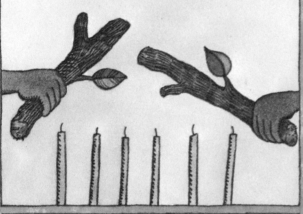

Make sure one is a match.

What did the boy with tangled hair say when he got a comb for his birthday?

I'll never part with it.

Why was the woman who baked the birthday cake a mean person?

Because she beat all the eggs.

What letter of the alphabet has the most fun at birthday parties?

U.

PARTY MAGIC

Be a magician on your birthday. Fool your friends. Here are some tricks.

Ask a friend if he or she would like four new quarters you can make yourself.

How do you do it? Just take a piece of paper and tear it into four equal pieces. Each piece is a *quarter* of the whole.

Say you have a magic pencil that can write any color of the rainbow.

No one will believe you. But you can. When a friend says a color, all you do is write down the word. When a friend says, "green," simply write down the word, "green."

Say you can write faster than anyone.

You can, too. When you have a writing race, you write the words: "faster than anyone."

You can do the impossible. You can leave the room with two legs and come back with six legs.

It's easy. Just come back with a chair.

Place three chairs in a row. Ask a friend to take his or her shoes off, and jump over them.

Your friend can't do it. But you can. It's easy to jump over your friend's shoes.

Say to a friend, "I'll bet you can't take off your shoes alone."

He'll say, "I can." But he can't. Not if you take off your shoes at the same time.

Put yourself through a keyhole. Or under a closed door.

All you do is write your name on a small piece of paper and slip it through.

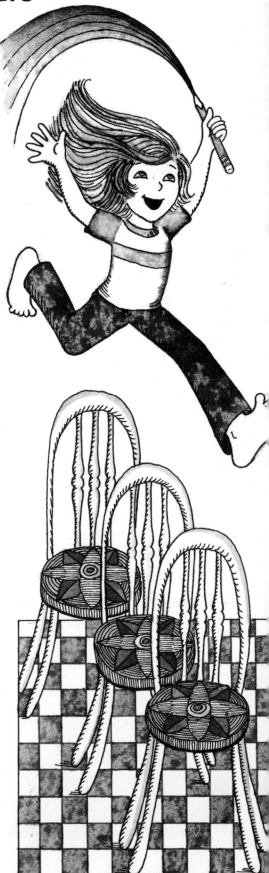

66

Here are some "mind reading" magic tricks that are played with a partner.

The magician seems to guess the right number by reading his partner's mind. The answers really come from secret signals given the "mind reader" by his partner.

Magic Numbers: The magician goes out of the room. The partner stays with the guests.

☆ The guests choose a number. Then the magician is called back. The partner calls out different numbers. When the chosen number is called, the magician says, "That's it!"

How does he know which is the right number? His partner's first question gives it away. If the partner asks, "Is it 23?" the magician adds two and three. Now he knows that the fifth number will be the right one.

☆ *Nine in a Line*: Nine things are lined up in a row. The magician leaves the room and the group picks out one object.

The magician comes back and the partner points to an object that was *not* chosen. The magician says, "That's not it." When he says, *"No, that's not it,"* that's the signal for the partner to point to the chosen object next.

☆ *Three in a Row*: In this mind-reading trick there are three objects and a secret silent partner. One object is chosen when the "mind reader" is out of the room. When he or she comes back, the "mind reader" points to the chosen object right away. It seems like magic.

It really isn't. The silent partner uses a signal to tell the "mind reader" which of the three objects is the chosen one. Right hand on chin means the chosen object is the one on the right. Left hand on chin means it is on the left. If the partner's hand is not anywhere near his face, the object is in the middle.

BIRTHDAY RHYME TIME

Fill in the missing rhyming word to complete the birthday verse.

Today's the day!
I'm feeling gay.
What day's today?
It's my *birthday*!

It's fun to mix,
It's fun to make,
It's fun to bake
a birthday *cake*!

The candles are lit.
The cake's on its dish.
It's time to make
my birthday *wish*!

SURPRISE PARTY FOR PANDA
(Hidden picture puzzle)

Peter Panda is sad. He thinks all his friends have forgotten his birthday. But they haven't. They are giving Peter a surprise party.

Help Peter Panda find his 7 presents, 6 friends, 5 party hats, 4 birthday balloons, 3 dishes of ice cream, 2 plates of cookies, and 1 birthday cake.

BIRTHDAY GIGGLES

Birthday Girl to Mother: Do you stir birthday cake batter with your right hand or your left hand?

Mother: I stir it with my right hand.

Birthday Girl: That's funny. I use a spoon.

Mother to Birthday Boy: Son, I baked two kinds of cake for your birthday. Take your pick.

Birthday Boy, in horror: What's the matter? Isn't the hammer sharp enough?

Mother to Repair Person: I have a terrible problem. I'm giving a birthday party for my child this afternoon and the roof leaks over the dining room table.

Repair Person: Does it leak often?

Mother, sadly: Only when it rains.

Teacher to Birthday Girl: How many sides has a square birthday box?

Birthday Girl: Two, the inside and the outside.

Same Teacher to Birthday Boy: Do you believe in birthday clubs for kids?

Birthday Boy: Only when you can't make them behave with kindness.

Nosy Neighbor to Mother of Twins: If you were really a good mother, you'd take the twins to the zoo on their birthday!

Mother, sounding shocked: Why should I? If the zoo wants them, let the zoo come and get them.

THE WISH

By Alma Friday

Each birthday wish
I've ever made
Really does come true.
Each year I wish
I'll grow some more
And every year
      I
         do.

HOW TO MAKE YOUR WISH COME TRUE

Wear a penny in your party shoes.

Break a dried wishbone and make a wish. If you get the longer end, your wish will come true.

Find a four-leaf clover and make a wish.

Look at a load of hay, make your wish. Then look away. (Don't look back till the wagon is out of sight.)

Pick up a penny in the street.

Throw salt over your left shoulder, making your wish as you toss.

Keep a horseshoe above your door. Keep the open end pointing upward, so your luck doesn't spill out.

Pat a calico cat.

Walk around your chair three times before you sit down at the birthday table.

Blow out all the candles on your birthday cake with one blow.

Wish on an eyelash that's fallen out. Blow it away to make the wish come true.

See a white horse, make a wish.

Find the one white hair on a black cat. Wish on it.

Catch a glassful of rain water. What you wish while drinking it, will happen.

See a redbird. Wish to see someone before it flies away. You will.

Count nine stars for nine nights, then make your wish. (One cloudy night and you have to start all over.)

Wish on the first evening star. Say:
    Star light, star bright,
    First star I've seen tonight.
    I wish I may, I wish I might
    Have the wish I wish tonight.
(To double your luck, don't say a word till you see the second star.)

PETER'S PET

By Sara Streander Lane

"I wish I had a pet," said Peter one day. "I've wanted one for a long time."

"What kind of a pet would you like?" his mother asked.

"I haven't decided yet," Peter said slowly, "maybe an alligator."

"An alligator!" Mother exclaimed. "Whatever would you do with an alligator?"

"On nice days, we could go walking in the park," Peter said.

"No, Peter." Mother shook her head. "Alligators have such big teeth! I don't think an alligator is the right kind of pet for a small boy."

"Well, what about a lion?" Peter said.

"A lion?" Father said. "Whatever would you do with a lion?"

"I could teach him tricks. Someday I could have my very own circus."

"No, Peter," Father said. "Lions are pretty wild. I don't think a lion would be the right kind of pet for a small boy."

Peter was very quiet for the next few days. His parents began to wonder what was wrong with him.

"I have a good idea," Peter said at last.

"What is your idea, Peter?" Father asked.

"Would you let me have a giraffe?"

"A giraffe!" Mother threw up her hands. "Whatever would you do with a giraffe?"

"I could tie him in the backyard. I could put a ladder up to his neck. Then all of my friends could climb it. We could use him for a sliding board."

75

"No, Peter," Father said. "A giraffe is too tall. I don't think that would be the right pet for you."

"Could I have a kangaroo?"

"A kangaroo! Oh, Peter, whatever would you do with a kangaroo?"

"I could climb in its pocket. It would be fun to leap around the city with a kangaroo."

"Peter, Peter," sighed Mother. "None of the animals you have asked for would be a good pet for you."

Mother stopped to think. "Well, you do have a birthday coming soon. Try to think of an animal that would be more suitable for a small boy."

"All right," Peter agreed happily.

For the next few days, Peter looked through all of his animal books.

Then he said, "Mother, Father, I know what I want. A bear!"

"A bear?" Mother was surprised. "Why, whatever would you do with a bear?"

"Well," Peter explained, "bears can roller-skate. I can roller-skate, too. And we could go roller-skating together."

"No, Peter," Father said firmly. "We cannot have a bear."

"How about an elephant?" Peter said. "Sometimes when I am out playing, I get very tired. If I had an elephant, I could climb on him and ride home."

Mother shook her head. "I'm sorry, Peter, but none of these animals is the right kind of pet for you. You will have to think harder."

"But tomorrow is my birthday," Peter said, "and we haven't picked out anything for me yet!"

"Well, wait until tomorrow. Perhaps there will be a surprise for you," Mother said.

Peter found it hard to sleep that night. He kept thinking about the surprise Mother and Father might have for him.

The next morning Peter woke up and shouted, "It's my birthday!" Then he ran into the bathroom to brush his teeth.

"I wonder if I have a surprise?" he asked the mirror.

He rushed back into his room to put on his clothes. All the buttonholes seemed to go on the wrong buttons. His shoelaces wouldn't stay tied, and his hair wouldn't stay in place.

Then *whoosh!* he was out the door and rushing down the stairs.

Mother was in the kitchen. He could hear the sounds she made cooking breakfast. There was no sign of a surprise.

Peter burst into the kitchen, "Do I have a surprise? Do I?" he asked.

"Of course!" Mother said, laughing.

"It is not in the kitchen," Peter's Father said, "it is out in the backyard."

Peter was already halfway out the door.

And there it was! It was small and round and fluffy. It had a wagging tail. It was a *puppy*.

"Oh, Mother, Father," sighed Peter happily. He lifted the puppy carefully in his arms. "How did you know that what I really wanted all the time was a puppy?"

BIRTHDAY COUNTDOWN

By Barbara Shook Hazen

1 lonely birthday child,
feeling sad and blue.
Someone's coming up the walk.
Now there are *two*.

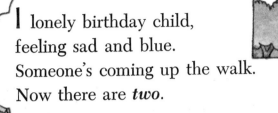

2 happy birthday friends,
sipping birthday tea.
Someone says, "Can I come in?"
Now there are *three*.

3 happy birthday friends,
playing on the floor.
Someone's peeking in the window.
Now there are *four*.

4 happy birthday friends,
trying to jig and jive.
Someone's skipping through the yard.
Now there are *five*.

5 happy birthday friends,
building a house with bricks.
Someone's mother drops him off.
Now there are *six*.

6 happy birthday friends,
wondering "Where is Kevin?"
Kevin calls, "I'm coming soon."
Now there are *seven*.

7 happy birthday friends,
swinging on the gate.
Someone's climbing up the back.
Now there are *eight*.

8 happy birthday friends,
having a wonderful time.
Someone's knocking at the door.
Now there are *nine*.

9 happy birthday friends,
drawing with a pen.
Someone's calling, "Wait for me!"
Now there are *ten*.

10 happy birthday friends,
giggling over a rhyme.
One laughs so hard his stomach hurts.
Now there are *nine*.

9 happy birthday friends,
eating ice cream and cake.
One says he's full and has to go.
Now there are *eight*.

8 happy brithday friends,
playing a joke on Kevin.
Kevin gets his feelings hurt.
Now there are *seven*.

7 happy birthday friends,
playing Pick-up-sticks.
One says she doesn't like the game.
Now there are *six*.

6 happy birthday friends,
feeling gay and alive.
One runs so hard she hurts her foot.
Now there are *five*.

5 happy birthday friends,
racing in the door.
One hits his head and has to leave.
Now there are *four*.

4 happy birthday friends,
sitting on a settee.
One hears her mother calling her.
Now there are *three*.

3 happy birthday friends,
wondering what to do.
One is bored and wants to go.
Now there are *two*.

2 happy birthday friends,
sharing a sugar bun.
One says it's getting late.
Now there is *one*.

1 happy birthday child,
who had a lot of fun
goes upstairs and goes to bed.
Now there are *none*.

BIRTHDAY BENNY

By Oliver O'Connor Barrett

This is the story of Birthday Benny,
Who wanted a pony but got a penny,
So he took the penny straight to town
To buy himself an Angry Frown.

He went to the butcher and said, "Mr. Brown,
Could you sell me an Angry Frown?"
"I could sell you a sausage or lobster tail,
But nary a Frown have I for sale."

Then he went downtown to the bakery.
"Would you sell me an Angry Frown?" said he.
The baker smiled and scratched his head.
"I don't use frowns in bread," he said.

Next to the hat shop went Little Benny.
"Will you sell me an Angry Frown for a penny?"
"An Angry Frown?" the milliner cried.
"You'll spoil your hat with a Frown inside!"

He said to the carpenter, "Mr. McGowan,
Could you sell me an Angry Frown?"
"Sure and beghorra, it is a shame,
But I've never an Angry Frown to me name."

Alas, poor Benny was in despair
As he crossed the wide and sunny Town Square.
Tears brimmed his eyes till he couldn't see,
So he walked straight into a little Nut Tree.

A Frown Mask tacked up in a high place
Fell down and stuck to Benny's face.
Then home he went, quite satisfied,
Wearing his Angry Frown with pride.

84

His mother was waiting at the door,
Her foot tap-tapping on the floor.
"That pony you left untied in the butlery
Has smashed the dishes and swallowed the cutlery!"

"A pony? A pony?" Benny doubted it.
"It's just what I've dreamed of!" Benny shouted it.
"You shall live in the parlor and sleep in my bed,
And eat candy and ice cream for dinner," he said.

Benny threw his Frown upon the floor,
'Cause it didn't fit him any more.
Then his mother went out, and with the penny
Bought cakes and cookies for pony and Benny.

And soon they were seated around the table.
The pony, as well as he was able,
Avoided swallowing fork and knife,
And seemed to be having the time of his life.

THE WITCHES' BIRTHDAY PARTY

By Frances Veirs

Once, and not so long ago, there were seven witches who lived together in a big dark cave. With them lived their seven fiery-eyed black cats that arched their backs and yowled, because they didn't know how to purr.

The cave was a gloomy place for a home, but the witches liked it that way.

The seven witches looked exactly alike and they all had the same name, the same nickname, and the same birthday.

The way they looked was just horrible, but the witches liked it that way. They liked their sharp faces, hooked noses and snaggle teeth. They liked the tangled hair that got in their eyes.

The real name of these seven witches was *Scatterfright* and their nickname was *Scat*. They had to use numbers to keep from getting mixed up.

Their birthday was every Halloween and, like everybody else, they liked to have fun on their birthday. They thought the most fun in the world was scaring people.

One Halloween, when it was getting dark and children everywhere were putting on costumes to go to parties, six of the witches were sitting in the cave, making plans.

Scat Number Two said, "I'll tap on the windows and, when the people look up, I'll make a horrible face at them."

"You don't need to make a horrible face," said Scat Number Five. "You look horrible enough already."

"Thank you," said Scat Number Two. "That is quite the nicest compliment I ever had."

Scat Number Four said, "I'll sneak up behind people on the street and nudge them in the back. Think how scared they'll be when they see me!"

Scat Number Three said, "I'll make myself invisible and I'll laugh a horrible laugh. Like this . . . heh, heh, heh."

Then the witches were quiet. They were thinking up more ways to have fun. And they were wishing Scat Number One would hurry back. No doubt she would bring them some lovely ideas.

At last Scat Number One came sailing in on her broomstick. The other witches could hardly wait to find out what horrible new things she had in mind.

"Tell us about your trip," they said.

Scat Number One sat down and looked dreamy-eyed. The other witches thought she must be sick.

"I saw the usual things," she said. "Boys and girls going to Halloween parties, calling, 'Trick or treat.' But the most wonderful thing I saw was a little girl's birthday party."

"*Birthday party?*" echoed the other witches. "What's a birthday party? Is it something more horrible than we ever thought of?"

"It's a cake with candles and pink icing,"

said Scat Number One dreamily. "And ice cream. And pretty little things called favors. And they played games."

The other witches were amazed.

But now Scat Number One surprised them even more. She said, "I'm going to conjure up a birthday cake with candles and pink icing. And ice cream and favors. Tonight we'll stay home and have a birthday party!

Then Scat Number One started conjuring. Instead of saying,

> *Shake and tremble, shake and tremble,*
> *Let the witches' brew assemble,*

she sang,

> *Happy birthday to me,*
> *Happy birthday to me,*
> *Happy birthday, dear Scatterfright,*
> *Happy birthday to me!*

Seven times she sang the happy birthday song. And then, on the big rock that usually held bitter brew, there appeared a lacy tablecloth, a beautiful birthday cake, seven dishes of strawberry ice cream, and seven little pink and white hats.

The other witches tasted the cake and nearly choked.

But when they tasted the ice cream, they decided this was even worse. Who could possibly eat anything *sweet*? The witches didn't want to be impolite, so they ate the candles.

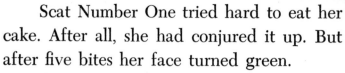

Scat Number One tried hard to eat her cake. After all, she had conjured it up. But after five bites her face turned green.

"Maybe the cake and ice cream will taste better when they're old and moldy," she apologized. "Anyway, we can put on our hats and play games."

Scat Number One tried game after game. Everyone looked sadder and sadder, with the dainty pink and white hats perched on their scraggly heads.

Then suddenly Scat Number One took off her pink and white cap and shouted, "*Great snakes and smoking cauldrons! Who wants to have a silly old birthday party!*" She went straight to the hitching post and picked up her broomstick.

The other witches let out a cry of joy. They were going to have fun on their birthday, after all. Oh, what a night for flying!

They would tap on windows and make horrible faces at people. They would sneak up on people on the street. They would laugh — heh, heh, heh — in people's ears.

And right away seven proper witches went sailing through the air on their broomsticks—with seven cats sitting in front of them yowling, and bats flying around their heads. They *liked* it that way.

HAPPY BIRTHDAYS AROUND THE WORLD

In Japan, the birthday child is given a colored bag of candy to bring good fortune and a long life.

In China, eggs are part of the birthday celebration. White for a long life. Red for joy. In China, the moon's birthday is celebrated at harvest time and round moon cakes are eaten.

In Puerto Rico and Mexico, there is likely to be a pinata party. A pinata is a colorful papier-mâché figure or animal filled with toys and candies. It is hung from the ceiling. The blindfolded guests take turns hitting the pinata with a stick to try to break it. When it finally breaks, everyone scrambles to pick up the goodies that have fallen out.

In France, children wear fancy hats at birthday parties. The more elaborate they are, the better. Hot chocolate is a favorite treat, musical chairs a favorite game.

In Thailand, children are given small animals like birds or fish, one for each year and one to grow on. The little animals are blessed and set free on the child's birthday.

In India, the birthday child is decorated with garlands of flowers. Giving, not getting, is stressed. The birthday feast is shared with the poor.

In Iran, the birthday child goes on a treasure hunt to find his or her presents.

In Nigeria, children celebrate group birthdays. A special day is chosen and boys and girls of nearly the same age celebrate a common birthday. The celebration is an outdoor feast.

In Germany, the guests often bring flowers rather than presents. A May birthday child is given lifelike chocolate beetles.

In Venezuela, the birthday child is sung to at school.

In Switzerland, a birthday tree is often planted when a baby is born.

BIRTHDAY MONTHS

Adapted from a book by Peggy Parish

JANUARY

Short days, cold days, filled with winter fun days. That's the month of January.

Snowsuits, boots, mittens, hats, scarves — such a bother.

Skating, sledding, snowballing, skiing — with lots of tumbles on the way. Maybe a skating party on your birthday. That's January.

FEBRUARY

February is the month for remembering. It is the month for remembering Lincoln's and Washington's birthdays.

That occasional mild sunny day in February helps us remember that spring will soon be here. But don't pack away your snowsuit. February is the shortest month but one of the coldest. Plan your birthday party around a warm fire.

MARCH

When the leaf of the oak is the size of a squirrel's ear, it's planting time.

The melting snows change the earth to mud. The March winds help make the earth soft and damp and easy to dig.

Think about a planting party on your birthday. How exciting it is to plant a tiny seed in the fresh earth. Spring is here at last!

APRIL

In April the earth sparkles with newness and color. Ladylike daffodils, giggly-faced pansies, shy violets welcome the showers which April brings.

Forest, field, and barnyard are alive with new baby animals.

Houses wear new coats of paint and birthday boys and girls wear their new party clothes.

MAY

In May the outdoors is calling for you to come out. Trees are leafy and want you to climb. Butterflies flit by begging to be chased.

There are so many things to find out. Is the brook warm enough for wading? Are the early berries ripe yet? Is it too early to have a birthday party out of doors?

JUNE

Everybody loves June! Vacation begins. The days are long and warm. And everybody is ready for fun.

June is a nice time to take a nature walk through the woods. Or take a trip with your parents. It's fun to see new sights. Some boys and girls celebrate their birthdays in faraway places.

JULY

Hot! Hot! Hot! That's the month of July. This would be a good month to be a fish. Underneath a sprinkler or in a backyard pool is a nice place to be.

But it's never too hot for a birthday picnic with fried chicken, potato salad, lemonade, and big slices of juicy, red watermelon.

AUGUST

August is the last month of vacation. Make every minute count.

Bears and other animals that hibernate are very busy now. They are eating as much as they can, before winter comes. Boys and girls are busy being outdoors, before the cold comes. August is the time for ice cream cones from the street vendor. An extra tasty birthday treat.

SEPTEMBER

How exciting that first day of school is! Seeing old friends. Meeting new ones. Hearing all about your friends' vacations and telling about yours.

The leaves begin to turn, and there's a smell of fall in the air. You might even have your birthday party at school.

OCTOBER

October is harvest time. Farmers hustle and bustle to get the crops in. Mice, squirrels, and chipmunks hurry and scurry to gather their winter food.

October is dress-up time. The trees change to brilliant reds, oranges, and golds. Children dress up for Halloween. And October birthday parties.

NOVEMBER

November is a resting month. The trees are bare. The flowers have faded away. The crops are gathered. Many animals nestle in their cozy dens. The farmers have done their work. It is time to rest.

November is also a month of feasting and thanks. Maybe you are thankful you are a November birthday child.

DECEMBER

Everybody loves the merry, hustling, bustling excitement of December. It is the month of happy holidays. Is your birthday one of them?

December is the month for spicy evergreen, burning candles, good things baking. It is the month for bells jingling and people singing. It is the month for colored lights and fancily wrapped packages. December is a happy month.

ON MOTHER'S BIRTHDAY

By Barbara Shook Hazen

On Mother's birthday she is not
allowed to fret or fuss.
Sis bakes the cake, I pass the plates.
Today the work's on us!

ON DADDY'S BIRTHDAY

On Daddy's birthday we've a big
breakfast with buns and tea.
He gets a lot of presents and
a birthday spank from me.

97

BIRTHSTONES, FLOWERS AND OUTSTANDING TRAITS

If you were born in	Your birthstone is	Your flower is	Your Outstanding trait is
January	Garnet	Snowdrop	Loyalty
February	Amethyst	Primrose	Sincerity
March	Bloodstone	Violet	Courage
April	Diamond	Daisy	Innocence
May	Emerald	Lily of the valley	Success
June	Pearl	Rose	Vigor
July	Ruby	Larkspur	Contentment
August	Onyx	Poppy	Joy
September	Sapphire	Aster	Intelligence
October	Opal	Marigold	Good humor
November	Topaz	Chrysanthemum	Determination
December	Turquoise	Holly	Cheerfulness

BIRTHDAY RECORD KEEPER

By Sara Coleridge

(Write the name and birthday of family and friends under their birthday month.)

January brings the snow,
Makes our feet and fingers glow.

_____

_____

_____

_____

February brings the rain,
Thaws the frozen lake again.

3   Mommy _____

_____

_____

_____

March brings breezes, loud and shrill,
to stir the dancing daffodil.

23   Julie _____

8   Pam _____

_____

_____

April brings the primrose sweet,
Scatters daisies at our feet.

24 Tammy

May brings flocks of pretty lambs
Skipping by their fleecy dams.

June brings tulips, lilies, roses,
Fills the children's hands with posies.

1 Jody Joy
11 Cindy Decatur
23 Lori Lucas

Hot **July** brings cooling showers,
Apricots, and gilly flowers.

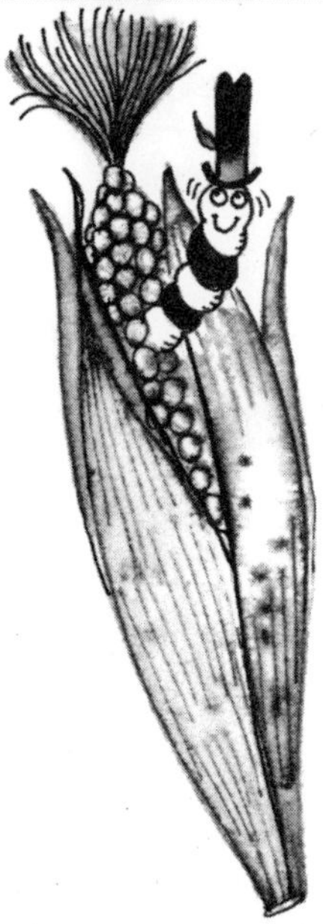

_____

_____

_____

_____

August brings the sheaves of corn;
Then the harvest home is borne.

_____

_____

_____

_____

Warm **September** brings the fruit;
Sportsmen then begin to shoot.

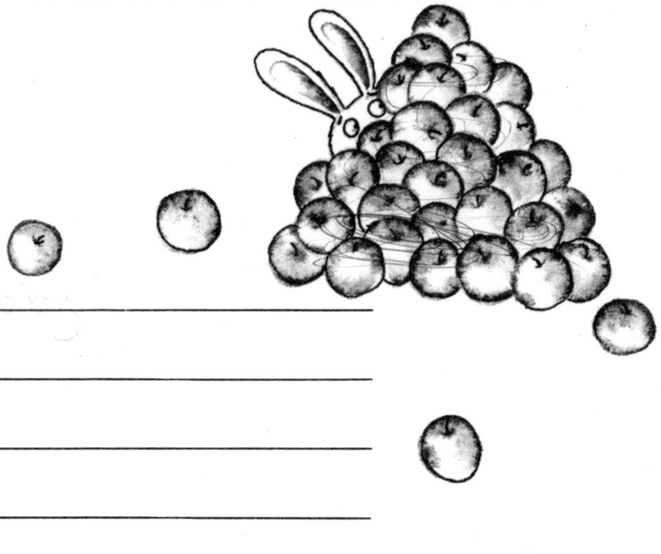

_____

_____

_____

_____

Fresh **October** brings the pheasant;
Then to gather nuts is pleasant.

22 Scott

Dull **November** brings the blast;
Then the leaves are whirling fast.

Chill **December** brings the sleet,
Blazing fire, and Christmas treat.

THE END

By A. A. Milne

WHEN I was One,
I had just begun.

When I was Two,
I was nearly new.

When I was Three,
I was hardly Me.

When I was Four,
I was not much more.

When I was Five,
I was just alive.

But now I am Six, I'm as clever as clever.
So I think I'll be six now for ever and ever.

INDEX